MEDIEVAL WOODCUT ILLUSTRATIONS

City Views and Decorations from "The Nuremberg Chronicle"

194 Illustrations

Selected and Arranged by
Carol Belanger Grafton

Dover Publications, Inc.
Mineola, New York

Bibliographical Note

Medieval Woodcut Illustrations: City Views and Decorations from the Nuremberg Chronicle
is a new work, first published by Dover Publications, Inc., in 1999.

DOVER *Pictorial Archive* SERIES

Library of Congress Cataloging-in-Publication Data

Schedel, Hartmann, 1440–1514.
  [Liber chronicarum. English. Selections]
  Medieval woodcut illustrations : city views and decorations from "The Nuremberg chronicle" / [edited], selected and arranged by Carol Belanger Grafton.
       p.   cm. — (Dover pictorial archive series)
  Includes index.
  ISBN-13: 978-0-486-40458-5 (pbk.)
  ISBN-10: 0-486-40458-7 (pbk.)
  1. Wolgemut, Michael, 1434–1519 Catalogs.   2. Wood-engraving—15th century Catalogs.   3. Chronology, Historical Early works to 1800.   4. World history Early works to 1800.   I. Grafton, Carol Belanger.   II. Wolgemut, Michael, 1434–1519.   III. Title.   IV. Series.
NE1150.5.W653A4   1999
769.92—dc21   99-26476
                                                                                        CIP

Manufactured in the United States by LSC Communications
4500051609
www.doverpublications.com

Publisher's Note

Nothing like this has hitherto appeared to increase and heighten the delight of men of learning and of everyone who has any education at all. . . . Indeed, I venture to promise you, reader, so great delight in reading it that you will think you are not reading a series of stories, but looking at them with your own eyes. For you will see there not only portraits of emperors, popes, philosophers, poets, and other famous men each shown in the proper dress of his time, but also views of the most famous cities and places throughout Europe. . . . Farewell, and do not let this book slip through your hands.

From Anton Koberger's advertisement
for the *Nuremberg Chronicle*

Of great historical significance in the development of Europe, Nuremberg was also one of the earliest and finest printmaking centers. Founded about 1040 by the German emperor Henry III, the duke of Bavaria, as a fortified settlement, by the thirteenth century it became a community of merchants and artisans, in large part because of its proximity to ancient European trade routes and its designation as an Imperial Free City. At this time, the distinguished artists Albrecht Dürer (1471–1528) and Michael Wolgemut (1434–1519; also commonly spelled Wohlgemuth), as well as many of their illustrious contemporaries, contributed to a flowering of the arts in Nuremberg unlike any before or since. And the proliferation of these artists' work was greatly facilitated by the presses of Anton Koberger (1440?–1513)—the most renowned German printer of his time—who helped elevate printmaking from craft to art.

With twenty-four presses and one hundred craftsmen in his employ, Koberger carried on a huge trade in books that were distributed throughout all the major cities of Europe. Although Nuremberg had other successful printers at work after 1470—the date when Koberger established the second printing office in that city—his large, ambitious volumes were of higher quality than any others published there. His two masterpieces were the *Schatzbehalter*, a religious treatise, and the *Nuremberg Chronicle* (in German, known as the *Weltchronik*, and in Latin, as the *Liber Chronicarum*), printed in 1493. The latter, issued just seven months after Columbus landed in the New World, was greeted as a publishing event, ranking second only in importance to Johann Gutenberg's forty-two line Bible (Mainz, 1453–1456) in the annals of bookmaking history.

Both of these historic volumes were illustrated by the painter and engraver Michael Wolgemut, with the assistance of his stepson, Wilhelm Pleydenwurff, another celebrated artist of Nuremberg. Some scholars believe it likely that Dürer himself (who was, incidently, Koberger's godson) was involved in the project, but others dispute that possibility with reference to the chronology of his whereabouts during the time of the book's production. Although Michael Wolgemut was one of the most prominent artists in 15th-century Nuremberg, and his workshop one of the busiest, his fame is most firmly grounded in his having been Albrecht Dürer's instructor in painting, engraving, and copper-plate engraving from 1486–90.

The *Nuremberg Chronicle* was immensely popular, and it is regarded by some scholars as the first major picture book for the middle class as it became a necessary addition to the libraries of the bourgeoisie. Thousands of copies were sent to booksellers all over Europe in various forms: it was produced in both colored and uncolored editions, and it was one of the first books printed in the "vulgar" or language of the common people—German in this case—as well as Latin. The text itself is a scholarly history of the world divided into seven ages—from the Creation to the discovery of the New World—mixing biblical, classical, popular, and political figures and events. It was written by Hartmann Schedel, a Nuremberg cosmographer and physician, whose ancestors dating back to the 5th century helped lay the groundwork for this world chronicle.

Since Koberger repeated many of the blocks several times, the *Chronicle* contained 1809 illustrations, with a total of 645 *different* cuts. There are various theories to account for the approximately 1164 repetitions: among them are the fact that it was a common practice for printers to do so in these times, to save money, and because many of the individuals involved in the *Chronicle*'s production had never traveled far from Nuremberg. In general, the views are more stylized than factual, with pronounced Franconian (Central German) traits reflecting many distinctive architectural characteristics of the site of the project's origins. Some scholars believe that the *Chronicle*'s woodcuts mark a visual revolution in the print medium from the territorial to the pictorial or landscape view—depicting the world not merely geographically with arbitrary yet abstract boundaries, but as a singular, conducive place for the traveler as well.

What follows is intended to be a generous and balanced selection of wood-cuts from the *Nuremberg Chronicle*. We have attempted to avoid repetition. When a single woodcut chosen from the original edition had been used to represent more than one area view, the other place names are referenced in the caption. Finally, thanks go to Tony Grafton and Stanley Appelbaum for translating the geographical references from their German source.

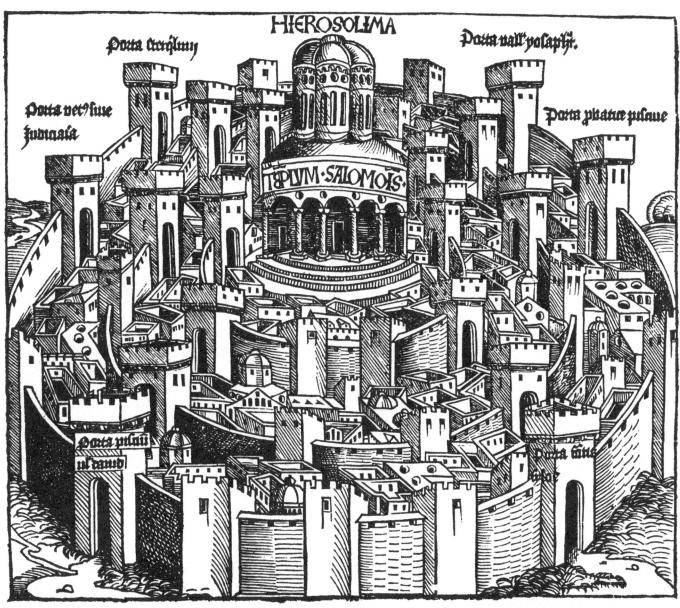

Jerusalem

Memphis (also Byzantium)

Sodom

2

Trier (also Padua, Marseilles, Metz, Nicaea)

Babylon

Damascus (also Perugia, Siena, Mantua, Ferrara, Carinthia)

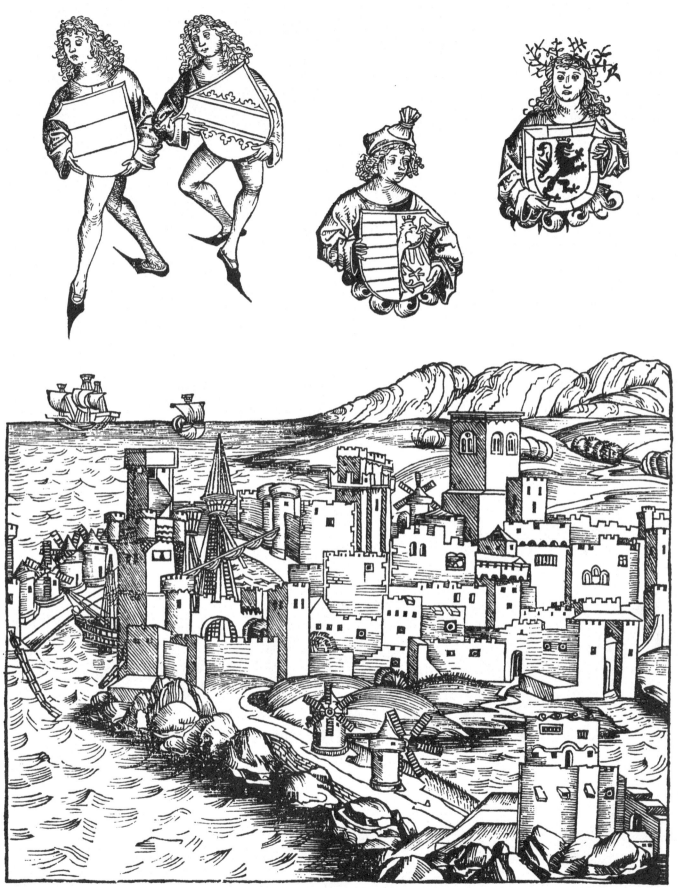

Rhodes

Athens (also Pavia, Alexandria, Damietta, Austria, Prussia)

Corinth

Troy (also Pisa, Verona, Toulouse, Tivoli, Ravenna)

Carthage

Mainz (also Naples, Aquileia, Bologna, Lyon)

8

ANGLIE PROVINCIA

Province of England (also Rumania, France)

VENECIE

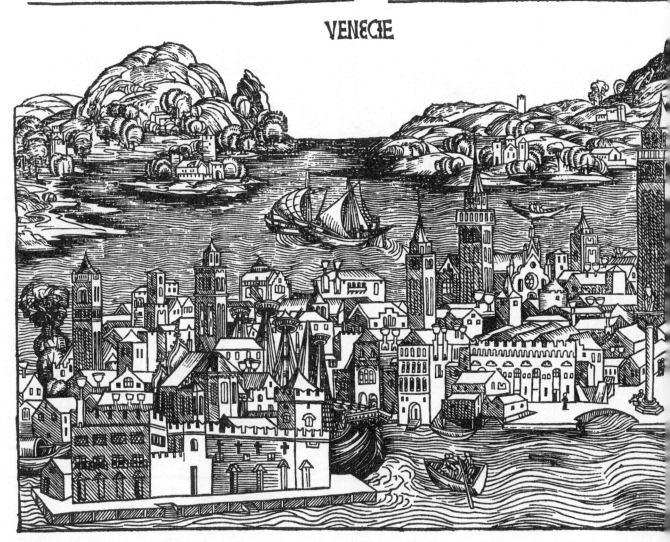

Venice

§ROMA§

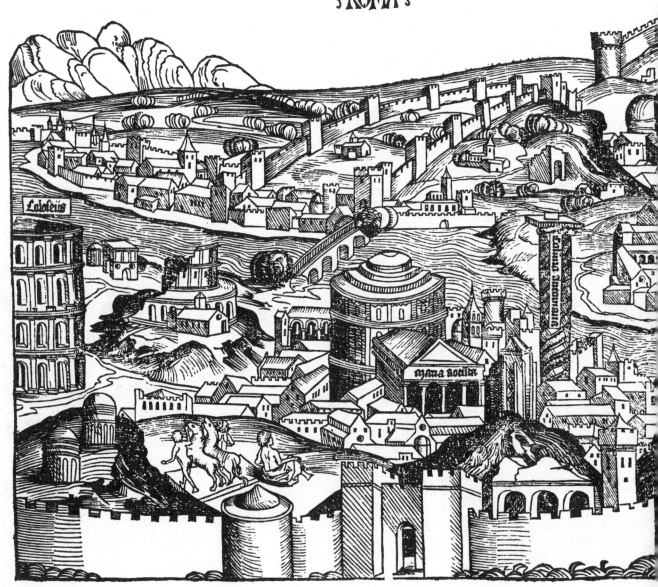

Rome

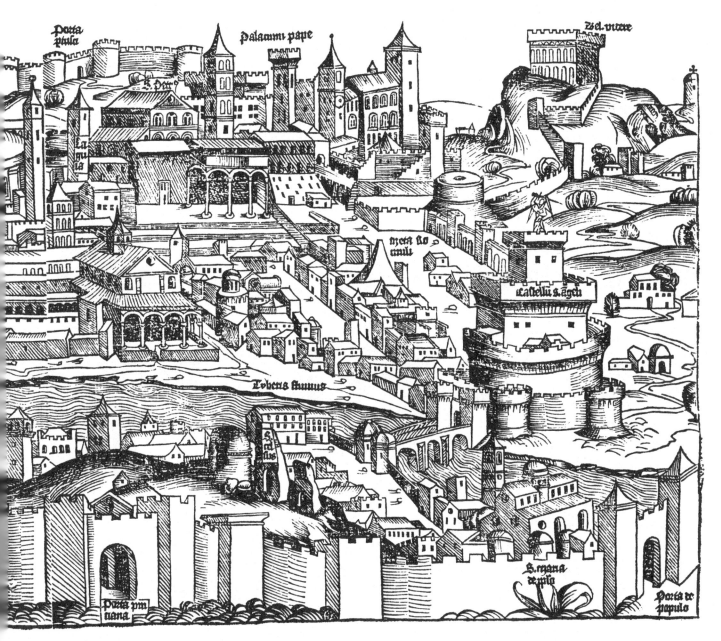

13

Babylon

Jericho

14

GENVA

Genoa

15

ĐESTRVCCIO? IHEROSOLIME

Destruction of Jerusalem

17

FLORENCA

Florence

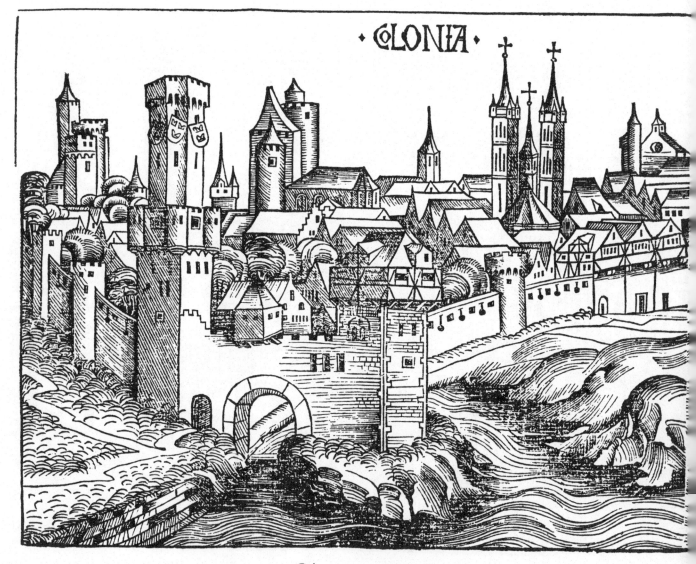

· COLONIA ·

Cologne

AVGVSTA

Augsburg

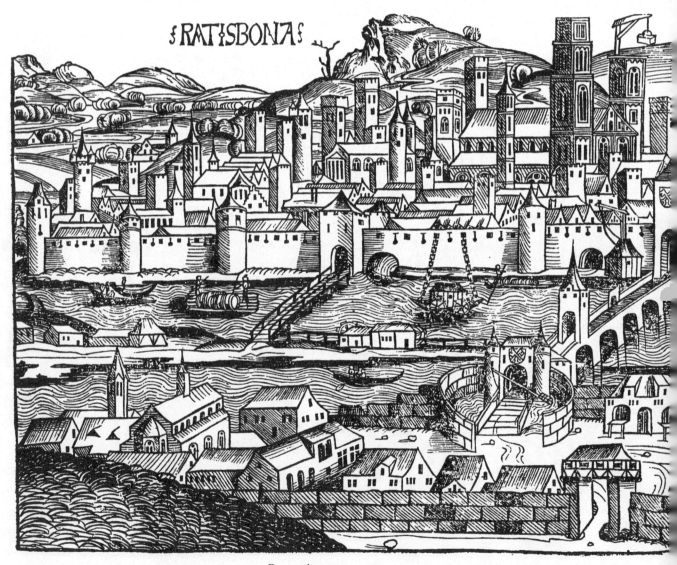

24

Regensburg

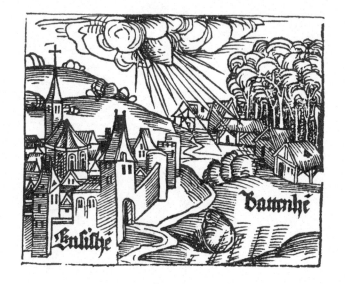

VIENNA·PANNONIE

Vienna

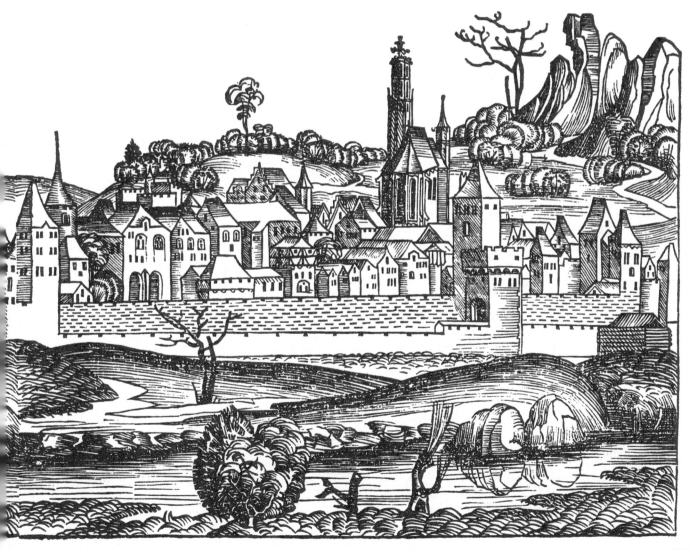

Nuremberg

Geneva (also Sparta, Tiberias, Milan, Poland, England)

Eichstätt

Constantinople

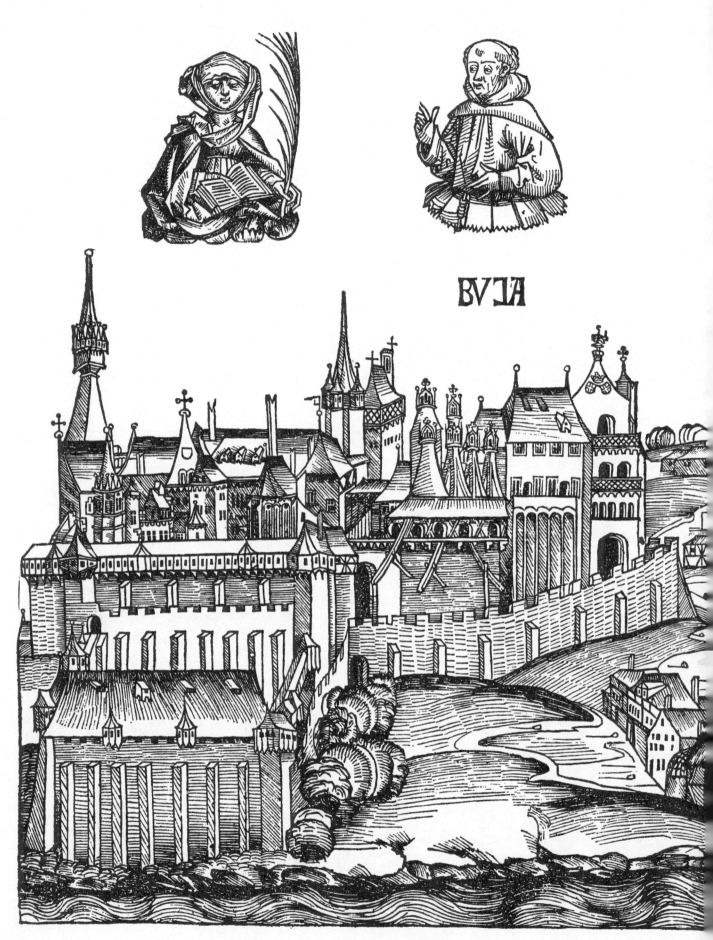

BVIA

Budapest

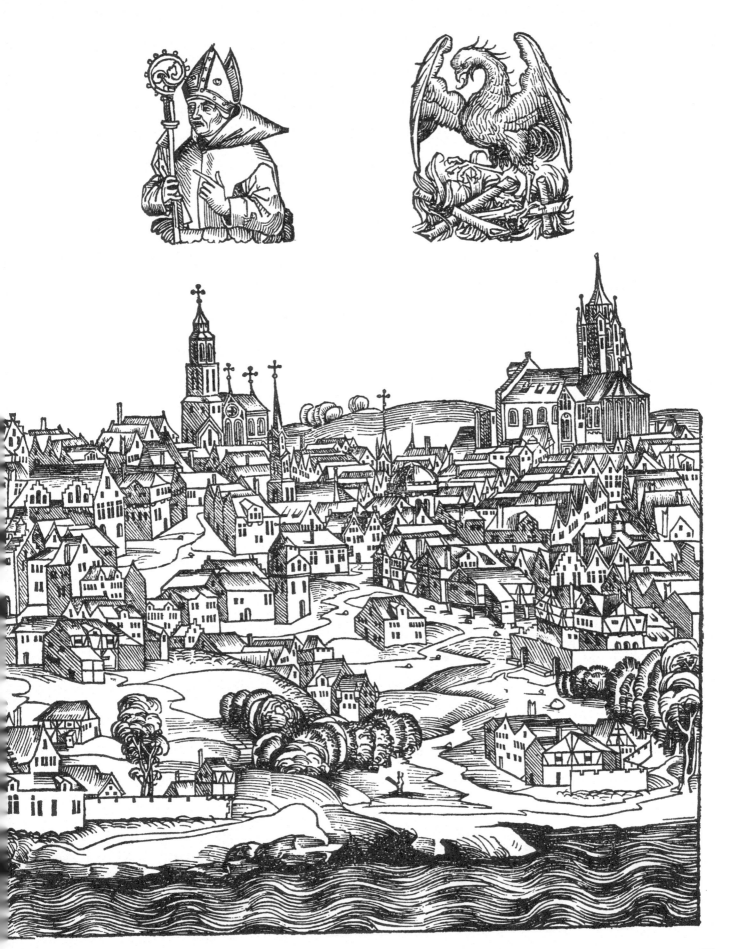

ARGENTINA

Strassburg

§ SALCZBVRGA §

Salzburg

ɀ ERFORDIA

40   Erfurt

41

HERBIPOLIS

Würzburg

§BAMBERGA§

Bamberg

MONS MONACORVM

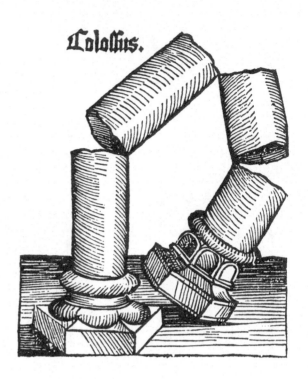

Coloſſus.

46   Magdeburg (left view only)   (full view: Paris, Treviso)

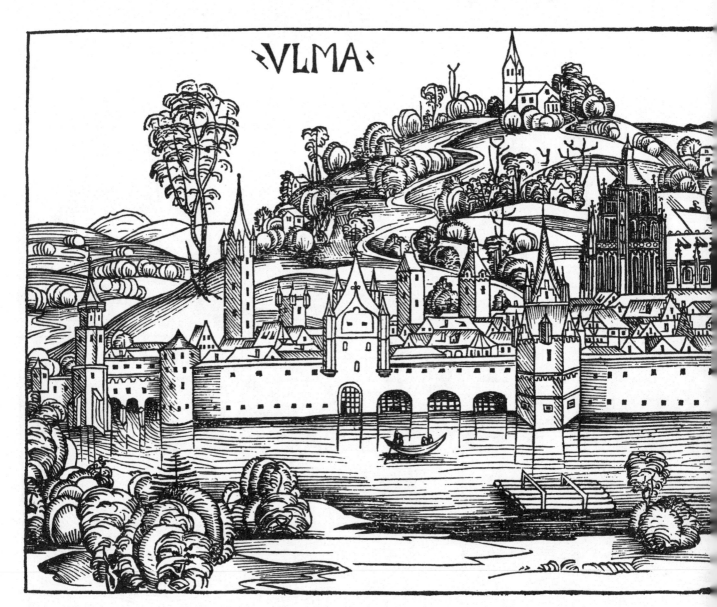

Ulm

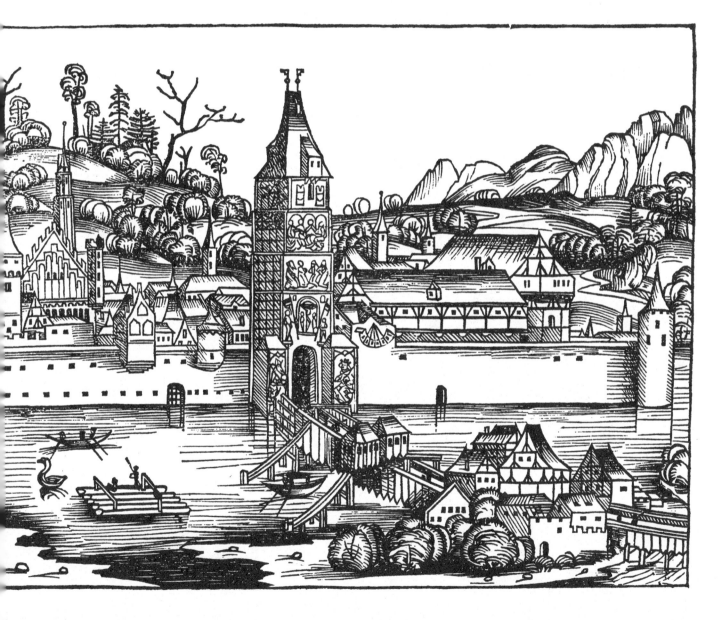

49

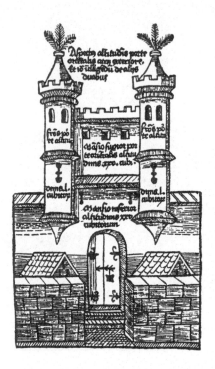

PATAVIA

Padua

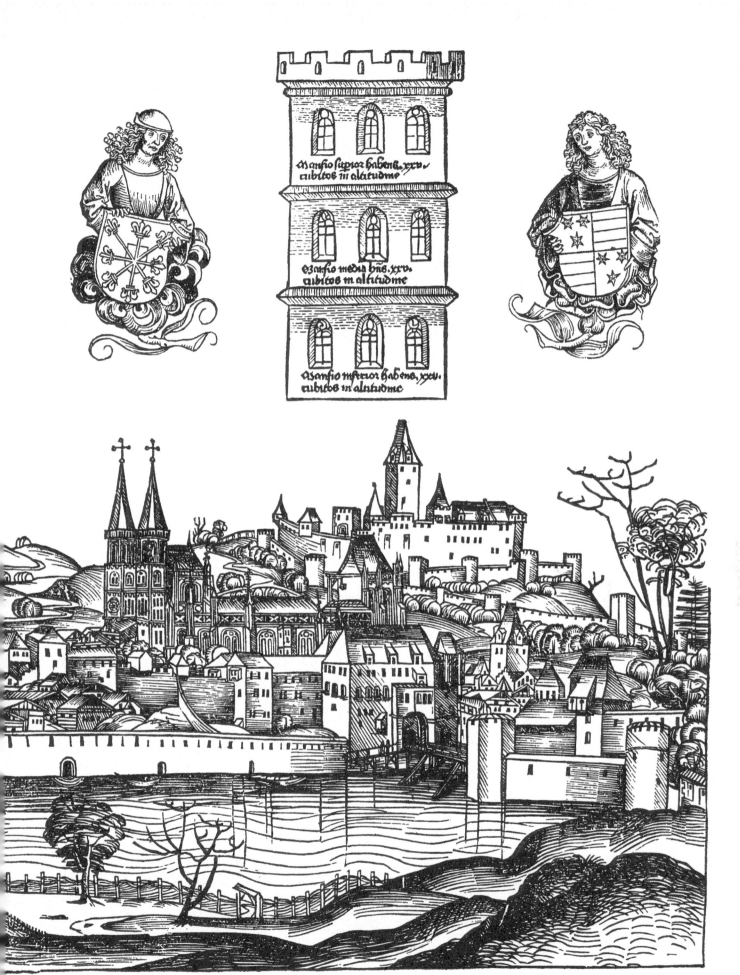

52   Munich

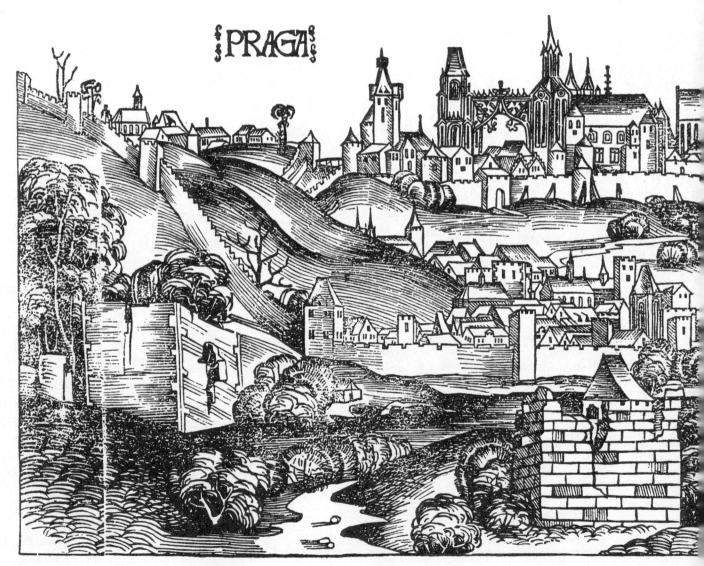

PRAGA

Prague

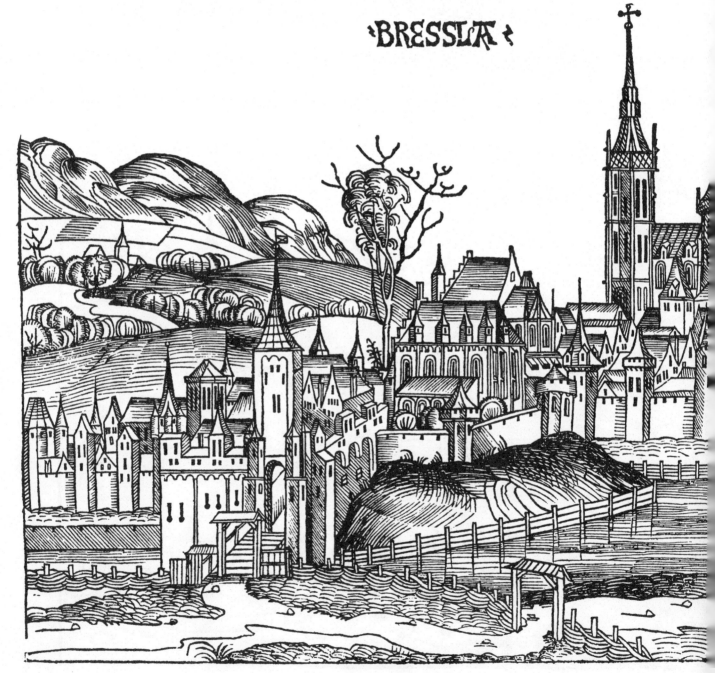

BRESSLA

Breslau

Konstanz

§ CONSTANCIA §

BASILEA·

Basel

60

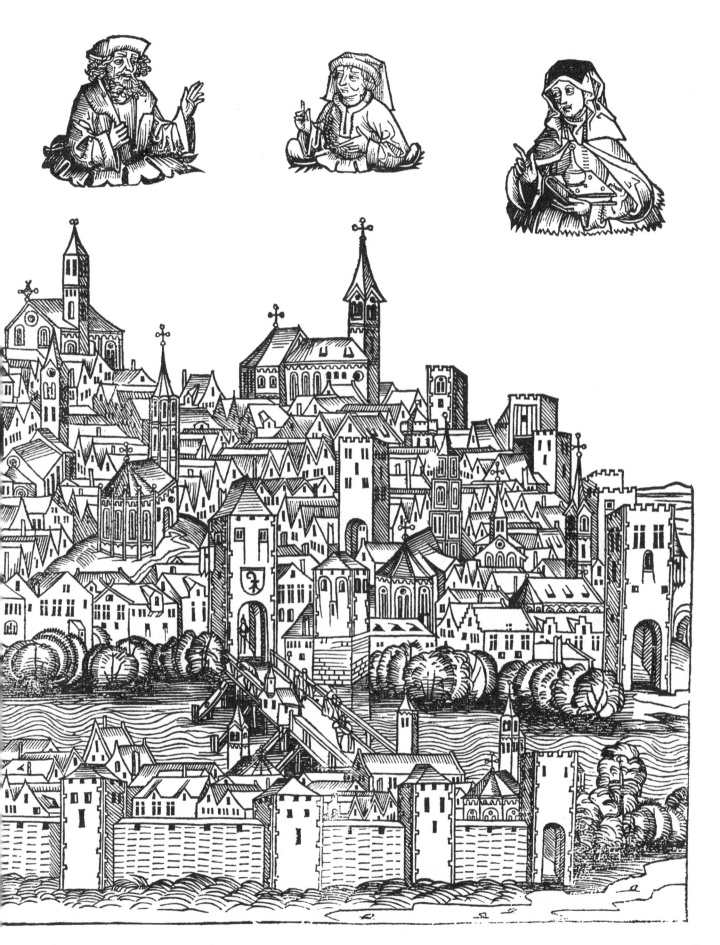

61

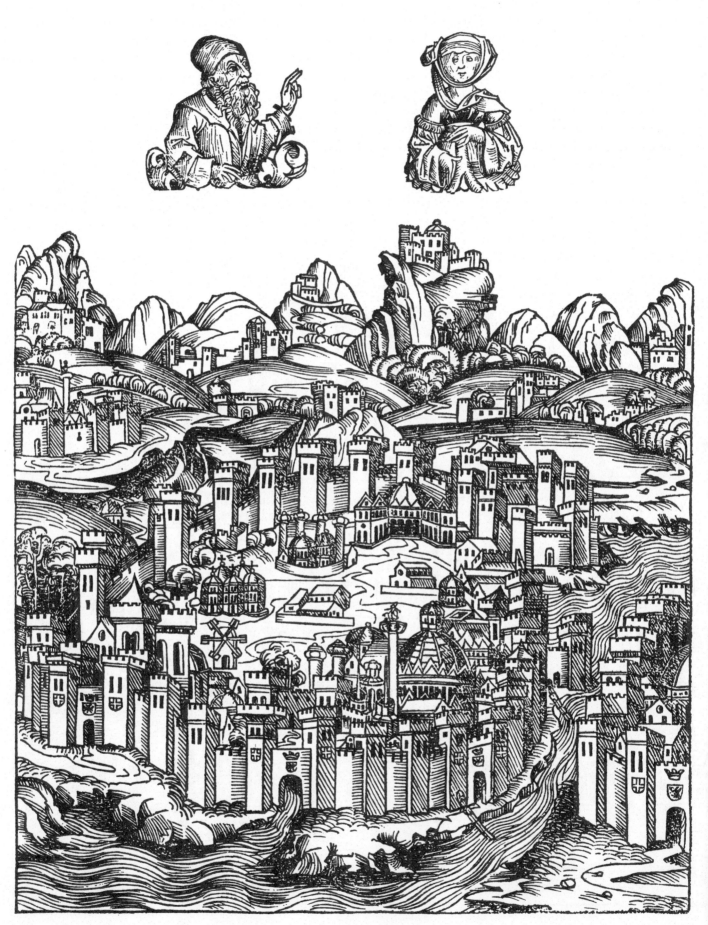

Constantinople

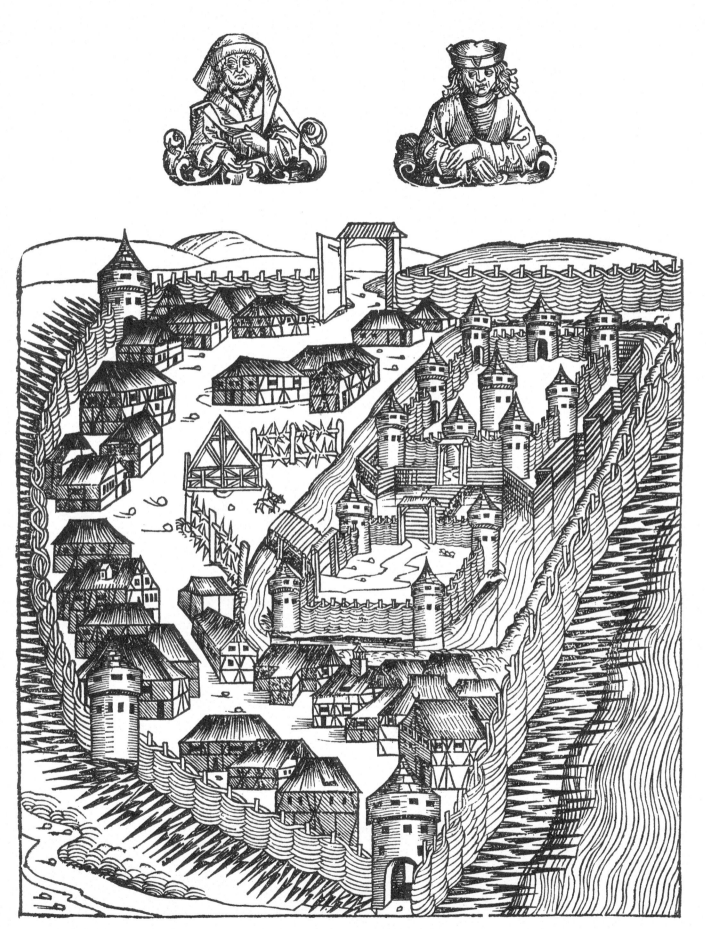

Sabac

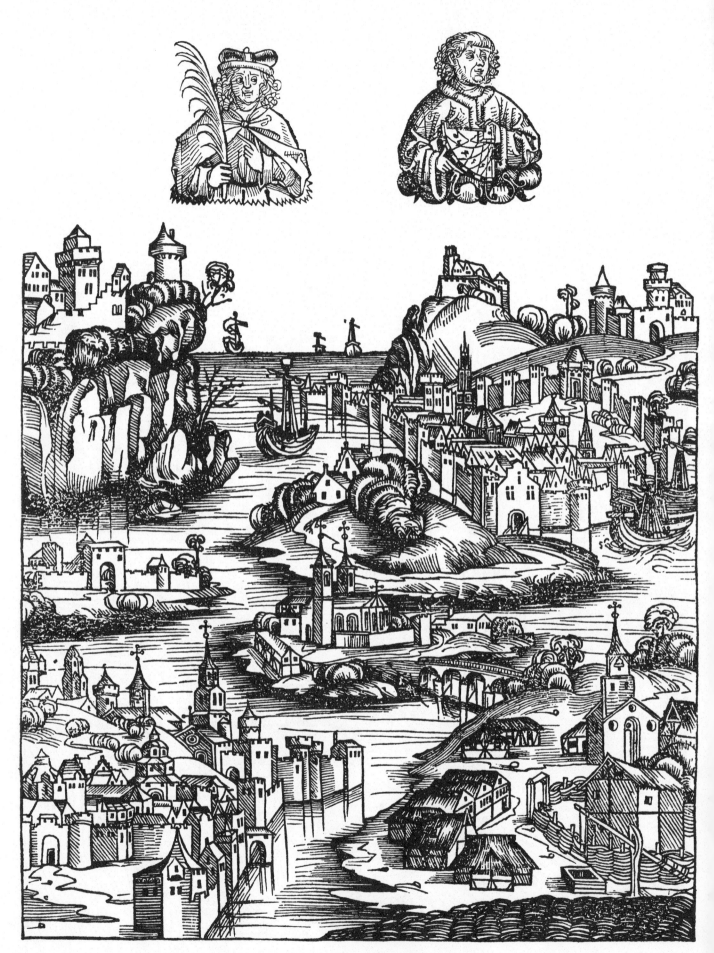

64   Poland (also Lithuania, Germany)

Hungary (also Thrace, Bavaria, Spain)   65

CASMIRVS

Cracow

CRACOVIA

CLEPARDIA

67

Lübeck

· LVBECA ·

NISSA

Neisse

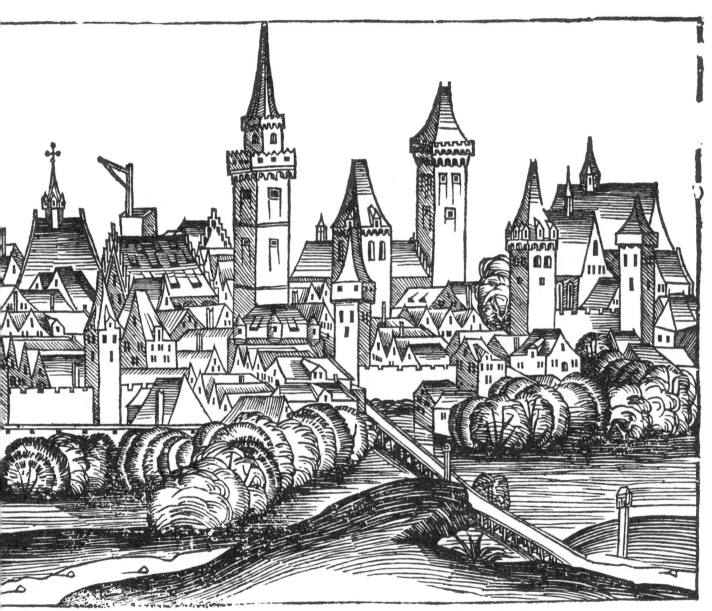

Turkey (also Saxony, Hesse)

Portugal (also Macedonia)

Index of Place Names

Alexandria, 6
Aquileia, 8
Athens, 6
Augsburg, 22–3
Austria, 6
Babylon, 4, 14
Bamberg, 44–5
Basel, 60–1
Bavaria, 65
Bologna, 8
Breslau, 56–7
Budapest, 34–5
Byzantium, 2
Carinthia, 4
Carthage, 8
Cologne, 20–1
Constantinople, 32–3, 62
Corinth, 6
Cracow, 66–7
Damascus, 4
Damietta, 6
Eichstätt, 31
England, 9, 30
Erfurt, 40–1
Ferrara, 4
Florence, 18–19
France, 9
Geneva, 30
Genoa, 15
Germany, 64
Hesse, 72
Hungary, 65
Jericho, 14
Jerusalem, 1, 16–17
Konstanz, 58–9
Lithuania, 64
Lübeck, 68–9
Lyon, 8
Macedonia, 73
Magdeburg, 46
Mainz, 8
Mantua, 4
Marseilles, 3

Memphis, 2
Metz, 3
Milan, 30
Munich, 52–3
Naples, 8
Neisse, 70–1
Nicaea, 3
Nuremberg, 28–9
Padua, 3, 50–1
Paris, 46–7
Pavia, 6
Perugia, 4
Pisa, 7
Poland, 30, 64
Portugal, 73
Prague, 54–5
Prussia, 6
Ravenna, 7
Regensburg, 24–5
Rhodes, 5
Rome, 12–13
Rumania, 9
Sabac, 63
Salzburg, 38–9
Saxony, 72
Siena, 4
Sodom, 2
Spain, 65
Sparta, 30
Strassburg, 36–7
Thrace, 65
Tiberias, 30
Tivoli, 7
Toulouse, 7
Treviso, 46–7
Trier, 3
Troy, 7
Turkey, 72
Ulm, 48–9
Venice, 10–11
Verona, 7
Vienna, 26–7
Würzburg, 42–3